Making Camp Gear

Making Camp Gear

Making Camp Gear

Camping: Where you spend a small fortune to live like a homeless person.

Making Camp Gear

11 Blacksmith Projects

ISBN-13: 978-1541263932

ISBN-10: 1541263936

J. A. Tuttle Co.

Table of Content

Introduction

Making Camp Gear is a straight forward how-to booklet on making these types of items to be used by the smith or sold. They are popular with the re-enactor folks and those who attend renaissance fairs.

I have made and sold these many of times. They lend themselves nicely to package deals and gift.

Hope you enjoy as much as I have.

James A. Tuttle

Managing Your Fire

Ring of Rocks   Set a ring of rock, dirt or heavy logs around the fire to help contain it and focus the heat to your cooking area. Burning inside a metal 5-gal bucket with holes in the walls for air would do the same. Try a 55-gal barrel for larger needs.

Dakota Hole   The Dakota hole is said to have been used by the Dakota Indians. While out in the woods or in the open this style of fire management produces less smoke, and leaves a small to no foot print. Dig a hole about 10" dia. And 12" down. Dig another hole next to it about a foot over and excavate a tunnel over to the bottom of the first hole. Wedge green sticks horizontally in the bottom of the larger hole, then good dry wood to burn. Once burning it will intake air supply from the bottom tunnel and pull down smoke through the smaller hole. This style of fire management was used so one could have a heat source without the fire light and smoke being seen by the enemy.

Swedish Torch   With one length of log about 18" long and about 10" diameter you can have an intense and focused heat. Split the log into quarters and loosely bind with wire on the top and bottom. Pack the cracks with pine needles, leaves and small twigs and ignite. The flame will burn vertically, sucking in air from the sides and

7

blasting out the top. Set you stew pot or pan on the top and you are set for cooking.

Swinging Heat   At some events the property owner/managers don't want burn marks in the grass of their fair grounds. You can eliminate this with a swinging pan to hold your fire. To make a quick swinging pan, cut the bottom of a barrel leaving the sides about 5" tall. Punch 3 holes, evenly spaced around the top edge to insert a chain's hook. Hang on a "S" hook from the center ring of your tripod with equal lengths of chain ending with a small hook.

High Fire   Another option is to prop the fire pan up on rocks or logs. Or if permitted, make the ring of rocks and fill it in with sand or soil. Remove the following day so not to kill the grass.

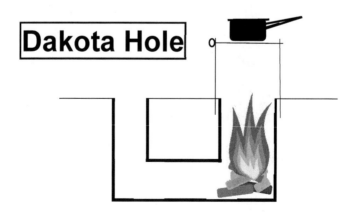

The Tri-Pod

This style of Tri-Pod offers two uses. First, it's a Tri-pod with an extra hook for hanging utensils or meat for cooking or smoking. Then secondly it re-assembles into a support rack to hang your pots and pans from while not in use and/or drying.

To make this style of tri-pod, start with 2 lengths of ½" round about 48" long. Heat and form an eyelet over the horn of your anvil. Give it about a 2" ID.

Next cut the third leg about 8" longer, in this case 56" and draw out a point. Let the taper of the point draw out about 2 ½" to 3" long. Heat the tapered point and curl as picture to create a pig tail hook. Let the eye of this hook be about ½" ID. Measure down from the top of the eyelet hook 3" and make a 180° loop with a 2" ID. Now the eyelet is upside down. mark the main shaft ½" above the now bottom of the eyelet, heat and bend to a tight 180° fold. Make any necessary aesthetic adjustments.

On the opposite end of all three legs, adjust to equal lengths as needed, heat and draw to a square point. This will facilitate sticking into hard soil.

As on the opposite page make 2 with the eyelets as at the top of the picture. Each eyelet will slide over the folded over top of the second leg in picture. The 3rd image in the picture shows the square point for each of the 3 legs.

Another style of Tri-Pod uses 3 legs of equal length each with an eyelet and linked together with a 3" ring. The eyelets are smaller, about 1" ID and the ring can be of the same material or lighter. Once the legs are spread out the ring needs to hang in the center where an "S" can hang from.

With this design the ring secures the three legs together and gives you a point to hang the trammel or other hooks. With this design, you can remove the ring and use as a pot hanger also.

Squirrel Cooker

Make a Squirrel Cooker for hanging lamps, cooking small game, sausage or Marshmallows. They are easy to make and are great gifts. These sell well at Demonstrations and Fairs when set up for folks to see how they work.

The Squirrel Cooker is great for back-packers. It has 2 components, the support and working rod. On the working rod, it has a fork end for cooking and a hooked end to hang your lamp or coffee pot. This rod simply hooks into the pig tail on the support rod and hangs your food over the fire.

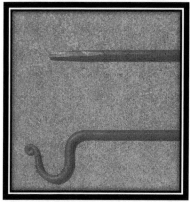 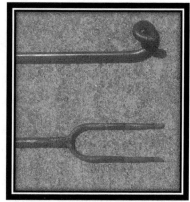

Start with 2 - ¼" rod about 24" long. Deburr one end, heat and wrap it around a piece of ¼" stock. Open the curl so the ¼" stock can easily be removed by twisting through the pig tail. On the other end heat and forge to a square point.

On the working rod, flatten 3" of one end. Using a sharp chisel, split the end, then fold the two fingers back to make a "T". Keep the material hot so not to lose a finger from brakeage. Heat one finger at a time, forge square then round. Now form over the horn or a hardy and bring the fingers back to form the fork.

To make the hook, draw the opposite end to a 4" point. Tap on the point over the edge of your anvil and create a tight curl to blunt the point and give it some style. Next wrap the tapered end around the horn or a 1" shaft to create a smooth and uniform hook ending in a 90° bend, as in the picture above.

Aline the hook with the fork to be at a 90° or in the same plane. Do this by heating the shank, place the fork in the vise and twist to the position you want.

Each way has its benefits. If you make it at a 90° to the fork you can hang small weight to counter balance the food being cooked. If you choose to make it in the same plane, it will pack better when laid flat in a sheath.

Finish the steel rod with bee's wax for a traditional finish or coat it with bacon grease and heat to cure the cook ware like a cast iron pan.

Camp Fire Grill

Build a light weight grill for backpacking.

The Campfire Grill can be made as heavy as you want to carry. A light weight version can be made from ¼" round rod for back packing. A more durable one could be cut out of $^3/_8$" stock.

A camper needs to consider what he/she will be putting on top if the grill. If it is heavy cast iron pots full of stew, then you will want to construct it from a heavier rod. Keep in mind, a large hot fire will warp and weaken a light weight grill.

To make the light set start with 10 to 12 pieces of ¼" round stock. Cut to 16" long. Make an eyelet on one end of each with a $^5/_{16}$" ID so it can easily slip in and out. Leave the other end blunt on all but 4 rods. The remaining 4 will be the up-rights that stick into the ground. Forge a square

17

point on each of the upright legs. For simplicity, make all the rods with square points so you don't have to search for the 4 legs.

To help carry the rods, make an 8" ring out of ¼" rod and thread all the eyelets on to it. An easier way to pack and transport would be in a sheath. Make a sheath out of canvas or leather. Fold over a strip of your material, sew up one end and one side. Give it a 5" flap fold over the end and tuck in for a closure.

For the heavier model, choose a $^3/_8$" or ½" stock. Remember to give yourself a little room inside of each eyelet.

Paint one end with High Temp Paint to aid in finding them all in the grass when you are packing up. Then wax the rest of the rods.

These rods are handy to have in camp. They also make great substitute tent stakes and can be wedged in or hammered into a tree to hang items on.

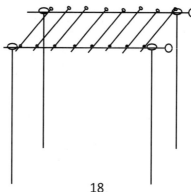

Single Pole - Grill & Hook

To make the Single Pole Grill & Hook start with $^3/_8$" round stock, cut pieces at 30" each. Flatten the ends of 2 rods to about ½" wide and 5" long. Heat and wrap around a piece of $^3/_8$" round

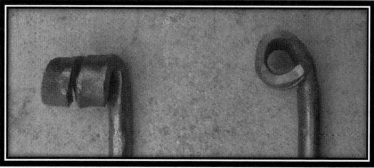

stock mounted in the vice. While hot wiggle and work the pigtail wrap loose so it will easily slide on and off a $^3/_8$" rod.

On the opposite end of each work to make the Grill first then the hook. Flatten out 18" on one end and split a burr off ¾" from the end, to make a decorative end. (Optional)

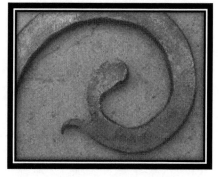

Bend the burr outward and out of the way so you will have room to shape the end into a tear drop. Start the tear drop by grinding the corners round or hammering them back. Then with a cross peen fuller in the side to create a tear on the end of the shaft. Now with scrolling tongs heat and bend into a flat spiral grill.

To make the hook cut the hook rod down to end at the edge of the grill. Taper the end and form a curl at the point. Start the hooks bend just short of center of the grill. Wrap the hook around the anvil horn

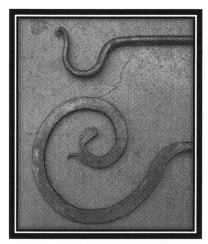

or a 1" shaft. You want the bottom of the hook to be at the center of the grill.

The 3rd rod gets a square point on one end and filed smooth on the other. Slide the 2 arms onto the shaft with the pig tails up. Adjust as needed to get the grill to sit flat and the hook at a 90° angle to it. For some customers, I have made a 3rd arm that is shorter. This one is used just for the counter balance.

When in use, the hook could hold a counter weight, like an un-used skillet to offset the weight of a steak on the grill.

Soup & Coffee Warmer

Made from black steel, brass or stainless steel this tool can warm your cup of soup, coffee or any fluid without having to pour it back into the pot. How many times has the pot been off the fire or maybe the fire has died out when you find your coffee has cooled. Setting your cup back on the grill may not be an option, but place one of these in the hot coals and then into your cup and its hot again. Cut 1/8" rod, heat and bend with scrolling tongs. One can set up jigs if many are to be made.

Any design will work, you just need a mass of metal to put in the fire and transfer the heat to your coffee.

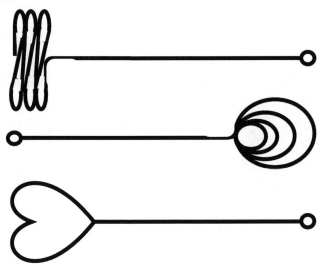

Trammel

The trammel is used to adjust the heights of hanging cook ware over the fire… temperature control. Suspended from a center hook on a tripod or a built-in swinging hook in a fireplace at home, the trammel is a convenience device and was often made ornately.

This small trammel is made from $^1/_8$" X $^3/_4$" X 12" flat bar and a piece of $^1/_4$" round stock about 12" to 14" long.

Drill a $^5/_{16}$" hole in the end of the flat bar leaving equal amount of material on all 3 sides. So, drill about $^3/_{16}$" from the end. Bend the end at about $^3/_4$" from the end to a 90° angle. Space out evenly 4 or 5 more adjustment holes. Snip off sides of the hook leaving about $^5/_{16}$" to $^3/_{16}$". Cut this about 2 ½" long. Heat then tap over the edge of your anvil to make a rolled-up tip, with scrolling tongs bend to shape.

Taper both ends of the adjusting rod. Form a hook over the horn of your anvil or hardy. Place the other end in the vise and bend to a 180° at 2 ½" then a 90° at about 1 ¾".

Thread the hook up through the bent bar eyelet and adjust the barb to be securely hooked into each hole. These may take a slight bend upward as seen in picture.

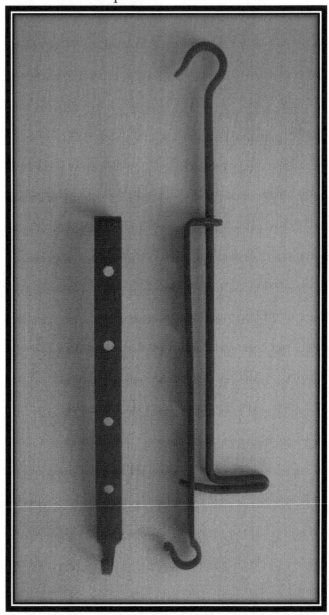

Trivets

At home on a good table or at the camp site where one doesn't want to burn the table. A trivet has been used for centuries to set your pot of hot food on. These came in multiple shapes and

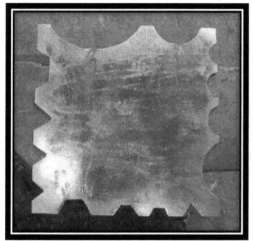

designs. Here are two trivets made as silhouettes of the trade. Small legs could be riveted, welded or brazed on.

You can cut them out with an acetylene cutting torch, plasma arch cutter, metal bandsaw, hacksaw, or metal snips, file, hammer and chisel. If you are out demonstrating the craft in the setting of the 1800's, or earlier, then the snips, hammer and chisel, files and a hacksaw would be in order. These trivets were cut out of 1/8" sheet steel. You could certainly use heavier or lighter material.

Some might wonder if these tools would be time-period correct. The answer is yes, the Romans had these tools during the Roman empire time. The Viking tool chest that was recovered in Mastermyr,

Gotland Sweden contained a hacksaw and metal snips. Leonardo Di Vinci drew a picture of a machine that would manufacture files.

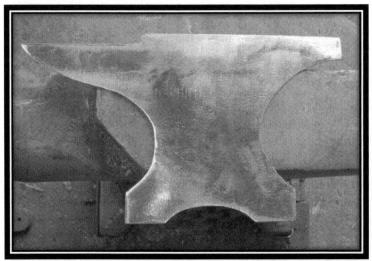

Other trivets can be made from simple coils of $\frac{1}{8}$" X $\frac{1}{2}$" flat stock. Coils would be easy and if you use scrolling tongs to twist the center into animal shapes it would make a more interesting trivet.

Let your imagination fly. Try riveting shapes and legs together to create unique designs.

Flint Strikers

When camping, you must have a fire. If you are a practicing survivalist or re-enactor the skills of using a flint striker is a must. A good source of steel for a striker is an old file. Other common options are old wrenches, chisels, and most any spring steel. Anneal it in your forge by bringing it up to a bright orange to yellow heat. You'll need to bring it up to its austenitization heat. Check it with a magnet while this hot, if ready the magnet won't stick. Return to the heat and hold the temperature there for 3 to 5 minutes. Remove and burry it in

some sand, ash or dirt to cool down slowly. Reheat and forge into desired shape.

Grind off the file teeth. If your file is tapered, forge into a rectangle then draw one end down to a point. Be careful not to overheat the tip and burn it off. Next draw out the matching end and after reheating it form the scrolled tips and wrap the

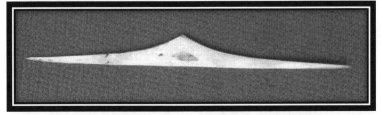

finger holes around a steel shaft of finger size. For a simpler version make one finger loop and cut off the blade at about 3".

Other Shapes

All that is needed is a flat surface about 2" to 3" long to strike along your flint. It is best to have your fingers away from the cutting edge of the flint, that is the beauty of the finger loops. But, if you pinch hard to hold them between your thumb and finger while striking, it will work. Try a pendant style bottle opener or one with a Rune

Stone marking that means fire. Stamping your Makers Mark on each would help develop your Brand should you want to sell more.

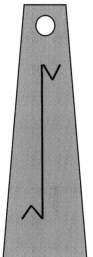

Tempering your Striker.

Once the desired shape is achieved adjust your fire to a level pot of hot coals. Break up any large pieces and insert the Flint Striker into the coals with the striking edge down. Raise the heat to the critical austenitization temperature again. Test with the magnet and quench in brine. Next set in an oven and heat to a tempering heat of 300° and to 425° hold for 2 hours. Let cool gradually in the oven then test for hardness with a file. Stroke the file over the striker with light pressure. If it is hardened the teeth of the file won't bite. Try striking it with a sharp edge of flint. It should produce sparks readily.

This process will harden your blades as well. At the end of hardening a blade, hone on a wet stone to bring up the best edge you can.

Char Cloth

To use a flint striker to start a fire you need char cloth. Place small pieces of cotton or linen cloth, old denim jeans work well, in a tin that closes tightly. Have one small hole for gas to escape from the tin, about an $1/8$" hole will due. Place in a fire for 10 to 15 minutes. Don't open until it cools after removing from the fire. If you open it while its hot, oxygen will come in and your char cloth will combust into flames.

To use, place the char cloth in center of your fire pit surrounded by jute rope fibers or other fine kindling. Shoot sparks onto the char cloth until it takes a spark and starts burning. Gently blow into the fire and feed it until it is strong enough to take larger pieces of wood.

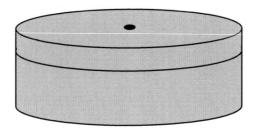

Cooks Prep Cutlery

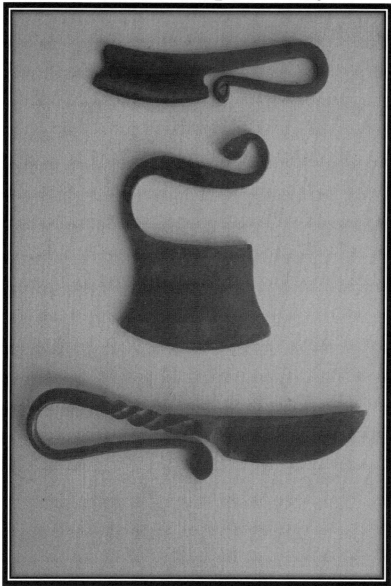

At the camp site, you'll need a good knife to cut up and prepare your food. A simple blade with the medieval metal handle or a more traditional handle made from maple or bone would work fine.

These examples of cutlery all have the medieval style handles. They were popular because if lost in the dirt and reclaimed later it is ready to go back to work. At worst, it only needed a little honing on a stone. Other handles would have rotted off and need replacement.

The process has been well gone over in my "Basic Blacksmith and "Next in Blacksmithing" book. But, to make a usable blade start with a file and treat it like making the striker above. Once annealed, draw out the handle then shape the blade. Put any twists and marks in it as desired then clean up the marks with a belt sander with a heavy to fine grit. Re-temper the knife and put the final hone on the edge.

Tent Stakes

Stakes are needed for many reasons.

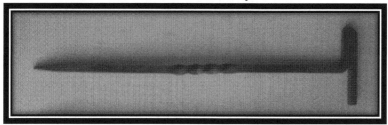

Obviously, stakes are needed for tents, but also its cousin the Fly and Awnings. They are used to hoist gear up into a tree to keep the wildlife out of it, and let's not forget the occasional need of staking out the family pet.

The Smith may be commissioned to make a set of stakes per the customer's design. To facilitate fabricating them, cut and mark out all that was ordered, then make all the bends making them all the same. This will help keep them uniform. If many more are needed, a bending jig may be in order.

When putting on a demonstration at fairs or re-enactments, the smith would be wise to make up some inventory ahead of time to sell. At lease cut several to length and make square points on each, leaving the top end to be finished per customer's choice.

Length can vary, as well as, thickness of the shaft.

Below are 3 stakes that are commonly seen and used by re-enactors and campers. The "L", "T" and the Cane styles. The lengths are per customer's order, but usually fall in the 8", 12", or 14" range and made from $^5/_{16}$", $^3/_8$", ½" square stock and Re-bar.

Square shanks in an "L" shape works great. Flatten out one end and bend to a 90° angle, then forge the other end to a square point.

The "T" Style is the easiest to pull up and with the added twist offers extra grip so it doesn't pull out of the ground while in use. Make the first bend at 6" then fold back the top 4" to make an even looking "T". Heat the center and twist.

Lastly, the lowly re-bar stake. Re-bar makes simple and cheap stakes which offers great grip on the soil. It only requires a quick bend around the horn of your anvil and a simple square point.

For this style of tent, 5 stakes per side is needed for the support lines, plus 6 more for the canvas. Prepare ahead of time to sell bundles of 16 stakes.

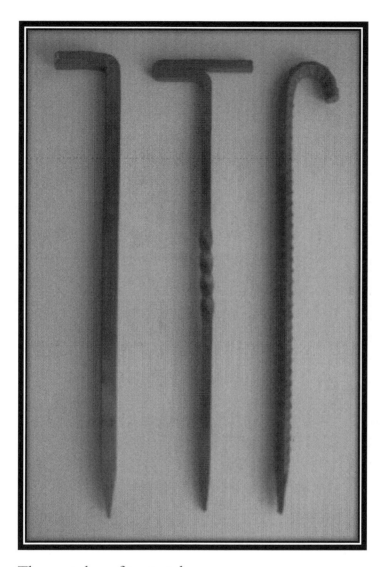

Three styles of tent stakes.

Under the shady pine trees my little smithy stands...

Made in the USA
Monee, IL
12 November 2020

47328673R00022